A Lot of Things, Kids

Quotes by

Victor Paul Wierwille

and

Others

Table of Contents

FOREWORD

Every person is the sum of all their experiences in life. We are all influenced by parents, siblings, relatives, teachers, neighbors and friends. Each holds a special place in our hearts. We are perpetually viewing others to pick up desirable traits to add to our life and discarding those habits and traits which we do not want to adapt. It is very rare that we find ourselves in a relationship that we so respect and admire to the end we voluntarily become their student in life.

In the Bible, Jesus Christ so lived and loved those around him that they referred to him as Master. He, Jesus Christ, invited his students into his heart. They were taught by him, lived with him, watched his every move and carried out his instructions. They literally learned, lived, loved, laughed and witnessed God's power.

In a similar fashion, many that were introduced to Dr. Victor Paul Wierwille chose to become his students. First and foremost in the Scripture and the work of the Ministry. But for many this learning process of a teacher and student soon grew into so much more. It grew into a father with his kids. These lifelong instructions and experiences included: from how to rightly divide the Word of God to how to eat healthy; from how to operate manifestations to how to balance a check book; from getting healed to how to heal others.

THANKSGIVING by THANKS LIVING is the greatest manifestation of being thankful.

The psalmist said, "Bless the Lord, Oh my soul, and forget not all his benefits."

No one can remember all of God's benefits, thus if we "forget not all his benefits," we will daily, moment by moment be thankful to Him for those benefits we remember.

I am so thankful that God's Word is God's will, knowing that I can only know the will of God if I rightly divide the Word of God. Having been led and guided of the Lord to know this, I am thankful that His Word means what it says and says what it means; that God has a divine purpose for everything He says, where He says it, why He says it, how He says it and to whom He says it.

Therefore, and for many, many more reasons, I AM THANKFUL.

Dr. V.P. Wierwille

Dr. Victor Paul Wierwille

LIFE

Breathe for God. He is the one that gave you that breath in the first place.

The difference between living, and really living the more than abundant life is detail.

If you're ever going to move with the greatness of the power of God in your life, you'll have to do two things: Speak in tongues much, and read and study the Word.

— Intermediate Class

We're always progressing toward something, either degradation or 'believers standing together'. Whatever we choose will end up in either life or death.

It's not important what I want to do in life, but what my Father would have me to do!

The whole gamut of life is wrapped up in the perfection of Christ that is within us.

The old man nature always pushes you to go extreme.

The nature of the human body is greater than the Devil.

It just becomes a life style for us.

Life without aspiration has no inspiration.

You can get lost in life more easily than in a forest. — *Life Lines*

Control your thinking and you control your life.

When you walk this life you don't go around and explain yourself. They wouldn't understand anyway! Men and women don't make your life, God does!

When the Word gains preeminence in our minds, then Christ is preeminent in our lives and living. Then the Word is life and then we are legally clasped in the hand of omnipotent love. — *(From Redemptive Living)*

The Word is the calling, that's why it needs to be taught.

I thank you for the privilege of making me a part of your life. — *(To the Sixth Corps)*

It's just not hearing the Word in your head people; it's putting it on in your heart and living it.

When you get to those deserts of your life, God will meet your need...Out there in the world, every place is tough...Love without courage is encasing. It's not how much money you make, but how much you have left over.

It's grace that saved and grace that makes it possible for us to live with all good words and works.

No life ever becomes great unless it is focused and then dedicated.

We've heard enough of the Word of God we need to act, people; we need to move. You know more of the Word of God than anybody perhaps known since the first century. So quit sitting on it, move — move. So why should we sit here until we die? And go to heaven or return or something and have eternal life? Why sit we here? We've got to move–move–move. We've got to live victoriously in life with the greatness of the love of God that's burning within our souls, people. — *Living Victoriously*

What difference does it make if history never remembers us, just as long as we remember in our lifetime to hold forth the greatness of God's Word?

Don't forfeit the more abundant life while advocating and promoting the more abundant life. When does anyone get enough love? NEVER! Therefore, the love of money is the root of all evil. 1 Timothy 6:10. Anyone who unjustly attacks and injures another must in justification of himself become that man's enemy.

Your body, soul and spirit all have to line up. It's very important to get to know your body and what it needs to operate the best. That's part of what the Corps is about.

The more you look at yourself, the more miserable you become. That's why to know yourself; the more you keep looking at yourself to know yourself, the more terrible you're going to feel. The more defeated, the more frustrated, the more doubts you're going to have, the more miserable you're going to become. But class, the more you look at God and His wonderful son, Jesus Christ in the light of the Word, the more joyful, the more blessed, the more dynamic life you will have because joy is an inside job. Happiness is dependent and determined by the things with which you are surrounded in the senses world. — *Living Victoriously*

Victorious living is living so fine
Living God's Word and making it mine
Loving the Father for sending His son
And running the race which is already won
Living the mystery which is Christ in me
I believed God's Word and then I did see
Just love to tell it and let it be known
What God did for all from His heavenly throne
Yes victorious living is living so fine
Living God's Word and making it mine.

— *Living Victoriously*

John 10:10

The thief cometh not, but for to steal, and to kill, and to destroy: I am come that they might have life, and that they might have *it* more abundantly.

"You put on
the love of God
in the renewed mind
in manifestation and there's
nothing you'll have to ask God for.
it'll be there. It'll be there.
You'll never have to ask --
it'll always be there."

LOVE

When you walk in the love of God in the renewed mind in manifestation, you won't have to ask for anything.

Loving giving requires loving reciprocal action.

All justice must be swift (I didn't say hurried) and tempered with love.

I sometimes think that what we call short-comings are really spiritual growing pains.

People are to be loved, things are to be used.

Love without obedience is hypocrisy. Obedience without love is slavery.

You overcome past negatives by present positives of love and truth.

"But as touching brotherly love ye need not that I write unto you: for ye yourselves are taught of God to love one another."
— *I Thessalonians 4:9*

You just got to get melted, people, into the mold or the cast of God's love.

God does not regard the greatness of the work we do, but the love and tenderness with which we do it.

The reason you sit and die is because you don't love people. Loving people means to do things for them.

Love must be enthroned in our lives in manifestation, it must govern our lives.

Man shouldn't contempt himself by doing less than the love of God in the renewed mind in manifestation.

Jesus Christ loved Judas; how much does He love us?

The only way your life will ever be pitched and in tune, if you have the love of God. Your life will never be in tune, it will never be pitched properly until you get it in alignment and harmony with the greatness of the love of God.

God sort of softens us up, prepares people and He keeps moving and moving. When you start seeing this in the Word, it builds a lot

of patience, love, forgiveness and under-
standing.

Calvary covered it all and that's why in God's
spiritual clinic, His greatest specialists are
heart surgeons who are transplanting the
hearts of flesh and stone with hearts of
love.

We have to have a lot of patience and love
with people. Whenever we get impatient, that
is sin.

We need a discipline out of love and not out
of fear.

Studying is a great aspect of life. It's a 24 hour
a day awakening to the love and grace of
God.

You see, any time you get close enough to a
fire, you get warmed up. You get close enough
to people with the greatness of the love of
God and burning in their souls, that love's
going to take hold of you and you're going
to be able to walk with it. So we have to
receive, and we walk and talk the talk, and
walk the talk. And we act the new nature of
the living Christ within us. We stay in God's

presence. We feed on God's Word, people, until our whole being is saturated with God's love. — *Living Victoriously*

Mark 12:30, 31

And thou shalt love the Lord thy God with all thy heart, and with all thy soul, and with all thy mind, and with all thy strength: this *is* the first commandment.

And the second *is* like, *namely* this, Thou shalt love thy neighbour as thyself. There is none other commandment greater than these.

MIND

It is the mind of Christ which is the key to our love life.

All we need to do is polish our minds with the greatness of the Word and let that Word dwell in us richly.

It's too big for the human mind, . . .but not too big for the believer's mind.

If you feed your mind on anything but the Faith of Jesus Christ, your thinking will always get out of control. — *Advanced Class*

You can't go beyond the persuasion in your own mind.

The senses cannot be renewed but can be controlled.

Control your thinking not to get out of bounds.

The mind is your perpetual battlefield.
                                        — *Advanced Class*

We are in the mind-blowing business.

Who do you take orders from? The head (Christ / the mind). — *Advanced Class*

Romans 12:3 – (Literal)

But I say to you because of the grace that was given me for all of you, control your thinking not to get out of bounds by feeding your mind with respect only to the measure of faith God has given to every man.

SPIRIT AND MANIFESTATIONS

Revelation is always specific if we could just sit it out and receive it. Stay still and let God finish.

To be bitter and resentful to those who criticize and find fault is for small men with immature minds who aren't busy thinking and working for more eternal matters.

If a believer does not act, he will never manifest the gift.

When you take the super natural out of Christianity all you have left is religion.

— *Living Victoriously*

The experience of the new birth is never biblically complete without some type of manifestation.

Revelation manifestations make available the MORE abundant life.

We watch out for each other by speaking in tongues.

Spiritual knowledge is ALWAYS RELIABLE.

Before we have healing, we must stand together to bring the spiritual temperature
up. We will never see great signs, miracles
and wonders until the believers stand together.

Once you really make Christ lord, that's when
you will be operating all nine manifestations.

There's a tremendous difference between
religion and Christianity, people. Religion is
based on human reason, human philo-
sophy. Christianity is based on God's divine
revelation. — *Isaiah 55:8-13*

It's not a question of owing anybody anything, it's a question of walking by the spirit
and loving people to the hilt.

Each situation is complete in itself and you
dare never read into it comparing it to a
previous situation which sense knowledge
wise looks the same. Revelation will be for
each individual situation.

Most of our dealings with people has been too
superficial in the spiritual. We need to operate the revelation manifestations.

God's got to give you revelation to teach you how revelation works.

Praying in the spirit is the greatest lever I know.

Every truth must fit in the framework of the manifestations.

God is spirit. Reach up and get yourself a handful.

1 Corinthians 12:1, 7 — (Literal)

Now concerning matters belonging to, determined by, influenced by, or proceeding from the Spirit, brethren, I would not have you ignorant.

But to every man is given the manifestation of the spirit toward profit to him ultimately as well as immediately.

FRUIT OF THE SPIRIT

The main thing in the Corps is to stay thankful, joyful, happy — to live it up and not get bogged down by some negative.

Christianity is a walk of exuberance, grace, joy, blessing. — *Advanced Class*

You will have fullness of joy to the end that you have fellowship.

We are the only academic institution I know of that makes its own joy.

Wherever there is a hardness of heart, there is a lack of peace.

Many who seem to portray themselves as preservers of the peace are in reality perverters of the peace.

Peace isn't something you work for, it's something that you have.

The more humble you are, the more you'll get done for Jesus Christ.

Galatians 5:22-23 — (Literal)

But the fruit of the spirit is: love, joy, peace, patience, gentleness, goodness, believing, Meekness, self-control. There is no law against these things.

BELIEVE

The spontaneous action of true believing is to await God's son from the heavens.

The Word of God is written for those who desire to believe.

You say it, you believe it, if it is according to God's Word, it has to come to pass.

Because all things are under your feet, you control exactly what you want to control by your believing.

We are what we are because of our believing.

The Gentiles were blessed by Jesus Christ in the same way unbelievers are blessed when believers are present today.

It takes 'silver-platter believing' to move the Word.

Without the Word of God, you just live in the consequence of unbelief. — *(Shared in Minnesota)*

Renewed mind believing is sanctification in manifestation.

God has never let His Word fall to the ground when men dare to believe it.

All through the ages God did His best to make Himself known to His people according to their believing. He desired a dwelling place where He could have absolute worship.

Two little words, on and in: We believe *on* the name of Jesus Christ for salvation. We believe *in* the name of Jesus Christ to live victoriously. — *Living Victoriously*

People, and that's us, believe what they want to believe.

The believer is the limit setter.

You can subdue and scale only if you believe.

Dreams become reality when we believe.

This walk of believing is as varied as the snowflakes.

You ought to be believing God for a big heart.

The greatest law in the whole world, which works with a mathematical exactness, with a scientific precision for saint and sinner alike, people, is the law of believing.

I do not believe that things happen accidentally. I believe that they happen because men and women believe.

For those who believe, it's the Way of Life; for those who do not believe, it's the way of death.

When you begin to believe what the Word says, your attitude will shake the world.

If you are ever going to win people to the Lord, you must believe in them.

Think of your life as the dropping of a pebble in a pond. The prayer of one man with believing affects the whole world.
...this is what the first century church taught (Ephesians) and believed — that's what made the church living and real.

— *(Ephesians 1:18-23 Teaching – 11/29/74)*

The word believe class, is a verb. A verb keynotes action. To say that I believe and then not to act is mental assent. Now both believing and mental assent are strictly in the mind. Believing gets the results of the integrity and accuracy of the Word. Mental assent simply gets the consequences of unbelief. A trick of the adversary, people, is to mentally assent but not act. — *Living Victoriously*

Hebrews 11:1 — (Literal)

Now believing is the title deed to things prayed for; the evidence they are yours before they are seen.

The Word Lives
Dr. Wierwille

THE WORD

Feelings come—feelings go.
Feelings, senses man deceiving.
My life and walk is the Word of God.
Nothing else worth believing.
Should all mankind the Word belittle and condemn,
I'll trust in God's unchanging Word until my very end.
Should man my soul and body sever,
I'll by God's mercy and grace continue to trust my saviour.
For God's Word liveth and abideth forever.

— *Opening of 34th Anniversary*

I just love to tie the Word around peoples' hearts.

It is just best to stick by the Word and shut up.

Thank you, Father, for our hearts being turned to you through your Word and your Son, like the sunflower to the sun.

Figures of speech are God's marking in the Word from Genesis to Revelation as to what God wants emphasized.

Don't complain to me. I didn't write the Book.

33

I am no different than any other man; I just pound the Word in my head.

Jesus Christ was the master of any situation...You never read about him having a need...The Word of God is the one thing in the world and the only thing in the world that will meet every individual's need — to his satisfaction.

True and accurate biblical and scriptural Christianity, people, is the one and only antidote to religion. For religion is the opiate of the people all over the world.

If the scriptures are silent, we dare not speak.

You've got to shake yourself up to God's Word.

We are being prepared to carry the greatest truth that any messenger ever carried — The Word of God.

People don't 'find Jesus', they are found of him, because the Word calls and draws them.

Sound doctrine will always produce fruitful witnessing. We cannot help but speak what we are, from the very fiber of our being.

Our approach and respect for the Word gives us that great lever of power.

You don't need a lot of people to move God's Word, you just need people who are knowledgeable, disciplined and committed.

It doesn't take large numbers of people to make things happen; it takes a few knowledgeable and committed ones.

VICTOR PAUL WIERWILLE
Life Lines

Drive the Word into your mind.

When the Word becomes the joy of your life, then you will manifest the more abundant life.

Anything opposite of God and His Word is death.

There is nothing quite as satisfying as The Word. When you're discouraged, go to The Word; and when you've blown $143.00, go to The Word.

I believe the only way to keep people moving is to teach the deeper truths in the Word.

Division comes from wrongly dividing the Word or refusing to believe it.

We have to teach the Word and nothing but the Word — but the Word *right now,* not ten years from now.

You're just as accountable to God for the practical way in which you manage your life, your time, your money and everything else as you are on the way you handle the Word of God.

Hold the Word in mind and act accordingly.

We have to declare the Word, even if it never comes to pass in our lifetime.

We may not know everything, but we're not deceitful.

I'm thankful for your love, prayers, notes and for the stand you've taken on God's Word more than anything else.

That's why you're in the Corps to develop that Word in your life. Think it through, dream it, teach it and learn to love with the love where with you were loved.

So, people, in your witnessing, don't ever get so serious that you think that the Word depends on you.

The greatest learning is in witnessing — holding forth the Word.

People who will not pay attention to detail will never be versatile with the Word. Unless you take care of detail in life, you'll never take care of detail in the Word.

You don't search the Word for the 'How to do' of everyday things. You get enough of the Word in you and it will manifest itself in the things that you do.

We don't have time to get sold out on anything but the Word.

The only media that does it is the taught and spoken Word. Read and believe the media of the Word instead of seeing, hearing, and believing the media of the world.

When there is no respect for the accuracy of the Word, we have to build it into people by building the logic of the simplicity of the Word.

We are not conditioned by experiences but because the Word says so.

Back up the Word, don't back up *on* the Word.

The reason people are so discouraged — because of the diet they're feed. They don't stay in the Word. They – you – spend more time reading the newspaper, the media and all that stuff rather than the Word, the Word. This is the greatest media in the world, people. The Word, the Word, the Word!

Theologians have expended more time and enjoyed more pleasure in their abstract theology than in their personal relationship with God. They have found more excitement in metaphysics than in the joy of His divine revelation in the Word. They have more pleasure in the opinions of men than the revealed Word of God.

I'm just going to bleed my heart out and teach the Word. That's what'll solve people's problems.

Whenever the gospel of grace and glory are separated, the corruption in practice begins and it culminates in corrupt doctrine which ends in spiritual darkness, decay and destruction.

There is nothing any bigger or greater than Ephesians and we're the only ones who know it and believe it. We have to drive ourselves to the point where we don't even have a doubt about its true greatness.

You never solve a problem by talking about the problem. You solve a problem with the Word, because the Word has the solution to every problem with which man is confronted. Get right to the Word from the beginning because it is the Word that meets need.

The Word changes circumstances because the Word changes people; and people change the world.

If you understand Romans, the rest of the Church epistles will unfold. It is the all truth, without distinction.

Religion has made the Word of God of non-effect by their tradition and that's why men today are living in deserts of spiritual despair and they drink from the stagnant pool of tradition instead of the fountain head of God's revealed and written Word.

— *Living Victoriously*

The now of the Word of God is so important that it could be called eternal new.

The great things happen in the inner chambers of the heart.

Do everything that is required of you in the Corps...PLUS. It's the PLUS that makes the difference.

Newness of life has no imperfection in it.

You know people, finite human language can

never fully reveal the infinite. For all words
are limited, thus I am constantly amazed at
the written Word. How these finite human
words that are so limited in order to fully
reveal the infinite, how God in His great
mercy and grace had men to write this and
how beautifully it has been written to com-
municate the greatness of the heart of God
even though God is greater than the written
Word. That's why the best that I know is to
always give the evidence of the Scripture in
the words of the Scripture and the sense of
the Scripture. — *Living Victoriously*

For most people Ephesians simply remains nice
words; you read them, you mouth them, but
never quite get to the place you believe
them. The Corps is supposed to be the
people who get down to the 'brass tacks' of
the Word and believe it. Even if you can't
explain it, even though nobody else agrees
with it, you still believe it and you operate it
and that's why there is no other place to go.

There are some people who know all of this
and they rightly divide a lot of the Word of
God, but their day by day living is not in
alignment and harmony with the rightly
divided Word. They know the rightly divided

Word; they even talk about it, but they don't live it. They talk the Word, but they don't walk the Word. You and I have got to not only talk the Word, but walk the Word. We gotta walk our talk and we gotta talk our walk, people. These people who know this rightly divided Word then don't walk it, they hold the truth but they are not held by the truth....You see people can hold the truth but the truth does not hold if they don't walk on it. — *Living Victoriously*

Small minds discuss other people — average minds discuss happenings — great minds discuss the Word. — *Christian Family & Sex*

I will not rest till every man has the chance to hear the accuracy of God's Word.

Psalm 119:11

Thy word have I hid in mine heart, that I might not sin against thee.

PROSPERITY

When we abundantly share, God promises to keep the devil from destroying in the future the innermost desires and longing of your heart. — *Christians Should Be Prosperous*

There are those who have no money, then there are those who have no need.

You can never out-give God.

And God is able to make all grace abound toward you; that ye, always having all

Sufficiency in all things, may abound to every good work:

II Corinthians 9:8

3 John 2

Beloved, I wish above all things that thou mayest prosper and be in health, even as thy soul prospereth.

LEADERSHIP

If you're going to lead people, you'll have to know how to inspire them.

Every leader knows he has limitations, but he doesn't worry about it; he just does what has to be done.

Inspiration will always precede believing by the teaching of the Word. . . .If you are going to lead, the first thing you must do is to inspire.

We'll always be following some type of leader. Just make up your mind who you're going to follow.

PFAL '77 will bring together the greatest leadership in the world today in a more intimate way than the Rock of Ages. I doubt if we'll know how great it is even when it's all over.

Anyone who has accuracy is a candidate for responsibility.

You cannot be a great leader until you can take orders humbly. Even when you're the top leader of an area, God will be giving you orders. People say they're tired of being given orders…Well, why don't you die?

You're only the leader or coordinator of people when you have their respect; and respect is something you have to build.

Leadership is common sense.

We are ambassadors for Christ now, not when we feel like it.

We have the ability to give people eternal life just by opening our mouths.

If you want constant confusion, go when God says wait.

We've got the TWO G's — guts and guidance.

Believe to receive, or doubt and do without.

Burn the bridges that you cross, and keep moving forward.

"Concerned" means to be determined.

The only way responsibility becomes easier is if we quit.

The success of fellowship is unity of service.

When God gives you an assignment, He sticks it out with you.

A twig that is blessed will continue to bless.

The harvest truly is plenteous, but the laborers are increasing.

Jesus Christ was the greatest salesman in the world — he sold out!

Mark 10:44
And whosoever of you will be the chiefest, shall be servant of all.

TEACHING

A true teacher is one who instructs so thoroughly and effectively that he is replaced by the student.

You need a few mountain-top experiences before you can minister in the valley of need....If you wait for thanks before you teach again, you'll rot in your grave. You teach because it's God's will and calling, not for men's acclaim.

Preaching is the basis; then you teach it.

The only reward you get out of bleeding your heart out to teach The Word, besides that spiritual abundance within you, is those people that stand with you.

Receive training in the whole Word so as to be able to teach others.

Our teaching platform is the world. Our teachers and speakers are you!

It's always easier to do something yourself than to teach someone else to do it as well as you.

And that's when he spoke to me audibly, just like I'm talking to you now. He said he would teach me the Word as it had not been known since the first century if I would teach it to others. — *The Way Living in Love*

2 Timothy 4:2

Preach the word; be instant in season, out of season; reprove, rebuke, exhort with all long-suffering and doctrine.

LIBERTY

Freedom is not maintained by fighting for it. Freedom is maintained by living for it.

Any nation that loses the true God cannot have anything BUT famine.

I want people to say: to hell with the Bible or to heaven with the Bible.

Freedom is WHO you are with WHAT you are.

Without God and an accurate knowledge of His Word, no nation can continue to be free.

It's interesting that people can always do things at the point of a gun, but can't do them with the freedom of the love of God. I think the Corps is what it's going to take to walk with the freedom of the love of God.

John 8:32

**And ye shall know the truth, and the truth
shall make you free.**

AMERICA AWAKES

If there is any one thing our country needs in this day and time, it is the Word.

The last vestige of truth—the United States.

The future of America depends not so much upon how many Americans hear the accuracy of God's Word, but upon whether or not those who hear rise up to walk in the greatness of what the captain of their salvation accomplished for them.

If our country is to endure and prosper, God's people must learn to live with God's ability so that His Word prevails and becomes the American way of life. This is what I call 'living in vital union with Jesus Christ' and this is what will bless America.

You are shooting too low! The governor needs it; the attorney general needs it. Go tell them 'Thus saith the Lord' or else they will die.

— *Advanced Class*

A thought for our country: Our times are such that our country desperately needs the healing love and enlightened guidance of God's Word. . . .I believe that if we will stand together as a family in one spirit, with one hand in the hand of God, holding forth the Word of Life like it has never been held forth before, we can move this Word across America. And then our country will have something to celebrate at the time of our Bicentennial Anniversary in 1976.

There is a tremendous spirit of excitement in our twigs around the country — lots of expectation. . . .

I'm blessed about the classes that are running, but that's just peanuts compared to what I see in my mind. There should be classes running concurrently in every community. . .all it takes is one believer who knows the Word and has the love of God in his heart to share it.

1 Timothy 2:1, 2
I exhort therefore, that, first of all, supplications, prayers, intercessions, *and* giving of thanks, be made for all men;

For kings, and *for* all that are in authority; that we may lead a quiet and peaceable life in all godliness and honesty.

**Word over the World Ambassador
Dr. Wierwille**

W.O.W.

In order for the Word to go over the world the light has to shine the brightest here.

When the Word is at work, then the Word will go over the world.

The Twig is the heart of all outreach of the ministry of God's Word, bringing God's deliverance to God's people before the gathering together unto him.

If you're ever going to move the Word over the world, and operate the manifestations of the spirit, people, you've got to get clear and concerned about the accuracy of God's Word and utilizing it in your life — it's the only way we can do it. — *Advanced Class*

Mark 16:15

And he said unto them, Go ye into all the world, and preach the gospel to every creature.

THE RESURRECTION AND HOPE

It is the hope of the return that allows men and women to go on, in spite of the negative situations and spiritual battles.

The reason Paul could keep going was his unalterable conviction and belief in the truth of what God was doing — the hope.

If I were not convinced of the literal return of the Lord, I could not stand the pressure of the ministry.

The first message given after Christ ascended was the hope of the return.

The resurrection is the whole keystone to Christianity — of truth. It ties the whole building together. — *Advanced Class*

HOPE — something we eagerly anticipate happening because *WE KNOW beyond a shadow of a doubt* that it is going to happen. Therefore we gear all our thoughts towards this event. This is being goal oriented.

Many men have been risen from the dead but they all died again. Jesus Christ is still alive.

The miracle of all miracles is for a dead person (Ephesians 2) to be born again.

The three darkest days in all the history of the world were the three days and the three nights when Christ was in the sepulcher.
Perhaps the three darkest words were: "It is finished."
But I know that the three greatest words in all history are: "He is risen!" — *Advanced Class*

It's the Hope that keeps you going with glory today, and joy and blessing.

The only reason a person has trouble giving is because he has no hope.

The resurrection stands as the great fulcrum of what God wrought in Christ Jesus. And that's why we're having an Advanced Class.

Without the hope of Christ's return, life becomes a drag for the believer.

You see, born-again believers hoping for something that's not available in the present, that's been the most beautiful type of spiritual failures I have ever known. Born-again believers who really believe God raised him from the dead, always talking about hoping for something that's not available, that in my experience in the ministry these years has been the most beautiful type of spiritual failure I know. There's always the battle between believing and hope.

— *Living Victoriously*

Christ's second coming has two basic phases; First is Christ's return for his church, the body, the gathering together where at that time we will have received our 'rest'. And second, Christ's return with his church.

1 Thessalonians 4:18
Wherefore comfort one another with these words.

THESSALONIANS

2 Thessalonians was written to reestablish the hope in the mind of the believers who had lost it because they were talked out of it.

2 Thessalonians; the model church of all the first century believers.

The key word in 2 Thessalonians in verses one through ten is the word "rest".

It was in 2 Thessalonians 2:1 that gave me my original guidance on the Twig.

He (the adversary) steals the believing of Romans from you. He (the adversary) kills the love of Ephesians, and he (the adversary) destroys the hope of Thessalonians, people. That's the adversary's tricks.

2 Thessalonians 2:1

Now we beseech you, brethren, by the coming of our Lord Jesus Christ, and *by* **our gathering together unto him,**

The glass is Christ ... the water is you.
  The water can't get out if it tries.
  It's restful especially at the bottom.
  The big waves are at the top of the ocean.
 Get deep enough in Christ and all those waves
 subside.

Yeah, well...a lot of things, kids

Put it all on the line, no compromising.

God Almighty, *El Shaddai*, means He is almighty in resources to defend, to support, and to supply every need.

In most other religious circles, they do simply the acceptable. We are not interested in the acceptable; we are interested in doing the best.

When I say 'reach up into Daddy's cookie jar' it's basically a matter of getting the cookie that He has.

Anything else than my absolute best is failure.
— *(regarding homiletics)*

Faith is the bridge that spans the chasm between the natural man and God.

In my heart and mind and from my knowledge of the Word, the greatest destruction I can think of is to be separated from God and His love and the fellowship of His believers.

People don't care what you know until they know you care. — *Life Lines*

A house is never a home until God in Christ in you lives there. The home is the heart of God. And the family is the background, the backbone, of the home.

Our example is a stronger inducement for others to serve God than any arguments about God's Word that anyone can propose.

Man cannot explain God any more than the Ford can explain Henry.

The greatness of the success of this walk is to do all things heartily as unto the Lord.

When you think you can't do any more then do it. That's what makes a winning ball club.

The greatest thing I know, the greatest truth that I know regarding Gods redemptive plan in the Word is that Father-God truth; secondly, the family and the household truth.

What the world calls frustration we call stepping stones.

We face the most difficult situations with an absolute sense of superiority;

We don't hafta 'got to do' nothing!

It's a new word, 'commititeer', a combination of a volunteer who is also committed.
— *Way Corps luncheon, Wichita*

One of the rarest things that a man does is his best.

People, as long as there is a family to stand together with, you just cannot stand alone!

You have to reach in before you can reach out.

The need was so great that I handled it the only way I know how — with complete honesty.

With righteousness, everything lost in the fall has been restored to us, plus. Righteousness restores spiritual initiative, confidence, assurance, fearlessness, and freedom from condemnation. When righteousness is restored, there is peace.

Christianity is the way of a Father with His family. God is our Father, we are His children.

Religion is the ways of men. Christianity is what God wrought in Christ, people; what He wrought in Christ Jesus and what He does in and for all believers. Religion is what men do to men.

Whenever and wherever a man is afraid of God, he will always be afraid of himself. When you see a man afraid of himself, there he is afraid of God. Our ministry is one of alleviating fear. Jesus Christ understood righteousness. – 1. He believed in God as his Father. – 2. That made it possible for him to believe in himself. – 3. He could then believe in the mission he had here on earth.

The least you can do is just give your all.

Quit riding the fence because it isn't there.

We want men and women who can hold forth the Word at the spur of a moment. — even amongst the Corps members.

To call yourself anything less than a conqueror is a sin.

People who can't be honest on time will be dishonest on everything else.

The product of sin disappears when sin is dealt with. Jesus Christ dealt with sin. He became sin for us who knew no sin so that we might become the righteousness of God in Him.

The family is only as sweet as we are sweet on one another. And we just want to stay sweet, right?

Our example is a stronger inducement for others to serve God than any arguments about God's Word that anyone can propose.

We need to know the Word in relationship to our culture.

In the Household you play no favorites.

Beauty, basically, is what you are on the inside.

Once a person arrives at the point of commitment, there's no stopping them.

Truth needs no defense — it needs a dynamic offense. In this class we'll develop a dynamic offense without being offensive.

The kingdom of God reminds me of a rainbow.

If there is anytime you want to be tender with people, it is at the time of death or sickness.

When you think you can't do it anymore, then do it some more.

You never rise beyond the goals you set.

We are not observers of times, but we do observe time.

God so loved you; therefore, you so *love!*

Don't give up if the pace seems slow — you might just win with another blow.

Failures are over with and unimportant, it's success that counts.

God chose us! Boy, the one thing I want to do is make Him proud of His choice. Sure, I blew it. But when I do, I go back and ask for another ice cream.

Retemories build a person's breaking point to a higher degree.

Religious leaders today don't talk any less about the Bible, they just say less.

A man once asked Dr. George Washington Carver, Who besides you can do these things? "Everyone can," said Carver, "if only they believe it." Tapping a large Bible on a table, he [Dr. Wierwille] added, "The secrets are all here...in God's promises. These promises are real, as real as, and more infinitely solid and substantial than, this table which the materialist so thoroughly believes in."

When I think of each one of you, I think that you're worth a 1,000 people if you've got the training.

The church for the most part, people, has simply magnified the historical Christ without the power of Christ.

When the hour is critical enough, you don't mind putting God first.

Unity without humility is hopelessly impossible.

We must develop a mental toughness to the point that we just don't budge on the Word.

We are a disciplined hard core group for the Lord Jesus Christ.

You've got a heart as big as a barrel, boy.

Trees are a lot like people. It takes years to build them but only seconds to destroy.

It's just as sacred to do sanitation as it is to mow the grass or study the Word under the apple trees.

People don't defeat us — we defeat ourselves because we don't look to the Lord, Let go and let God. — *PFAL class*

Jesus Christ didn't come to send people to hell but to keep them out of it.

Jesus Christ loved! He could have walked off that cross. — *PFAL class*

God never magnifies sin but the Savior from sin.

We never finish 'till the work is done.

You can be rooted without much ground. We're not to be surface rooted, we're to be ground rooted. — *Advanced Class*

If you're deeply rooted, you're gonna have a

few waves at the top of your life, but never at your foundations of conviction.

— *Advanced Class*

It's like you just swallowed 16 pounds of son-shine.

Man does not retard God's action nor facilitate it; in the fulness of time, he's coming back.

You learn by exerting yourself, self-honor, self-respect.

Throw your shoulders back, let them see a woman of God again, a man of God again.

This is not just a 'now' ministry; it is an 'eternity' ministry.

Adverse conditions are no excuse for failure to rejoice.

Respect yourself as the finest men or women of God the world has ever seen.

This ministry does not depend upon us but primarily upon God — our job is to plant and water.

We ought to so pull together that nothing can pull us apart. No one touches the family.

I have no peer but God.

Most people get strung out on the vessel, we have to get strung out on the treasure.

Believers dare never be indifferent to the impact that's produced by our example.

I allow people to walk on my feet because Jesus Christ allowed me to walk in his shoes.

Prayer is not so much in getting anything from God but getting you in tune with reality — (with God).

It's gotta' be burnin' in your soul honey before it can burn in anybody else's.

We will make the future as bright as the distance we walk now.

The greatest part of education is learning to think for yourself.

True education is preparation for living, not a means for making money.

We cannot bring the people to the mountain; we must disperse the mountain to the people.

All education is absolutely bankrupt without a knowledge of God's matchless Word.

You must be together with; then you can be together upon — together with God, then together upon His Word in the Corps.

The love of money is the root of all evil. It's possible for God to turn this captivity.

Our business is *first* the Father's business. We are businessmen of God and doing our business according to the Word.

Let the Word of God be the will of God. Never get so busy that God doesn't come first.

God is in business to prosper His men.

The reason we wandered aimlessly is because there has been no knowledge of God's Word. When there has been, there was no application of it.

No nation produces without the true God.

The only people who have a green thumb are those who have the growth of the Word of God.

Since we know the rightly divided Word, why not enjoy the greatness of the presence of God in people?

God softens people up. You must have a lot of patience and love. You can never get too much love.

I do not believe you can ever get too much of the Word of God.

Right now is always the greatest moment of your life; it can either be positive or negative.

We're in the business of planting and watering. Quit stewing about the increase.

Revelation is always specific if we just wait on it.

Remember: Boldness is freedom and frankness to speak the Word without fear.

Man would never be complete without the revelation of the Word.

The only thing that decreases as you get into the Word is the old man.

He gave his life for us: How can we do less? We only have one life to live.

It is the attitude in your heart and mind that affects your walk.

The more you speak in tongues in your private prayer life, the more dynamic your life on earth will be.

The more time you give to the Word, the more life you'll have.

We have life for today and hope for the future. — Where there is hope, there is no sorrow.

The spirit should be the foremost interest in our total being.

The moment the senses are permitted to rule the mind and body, instead of the spirit, calamity results.

Success is faithfulness — It's a privilege and honor to do God's will because it's for our benefit.

Life was made to be beautiful.

Never think about something you don't want to happen.

Stake your knowledge and trust in God, for He alone is your solid foundation.

Leap out, and God will never drop you.

When you run up against Jesus Christ, you have to make a decision.

Everyone believes what he wants to believe.

We must have separation of church and state, but not separation of *truth* and state.

We stand with that rock, Christ Jesus, within us.

You're either a stumbling block or a stepping stone.

What you think about Jesus Christ is what will determine what you do in your life.

I don't believe we are living by accident; I believe we are living by providence.

I just let God be God and I love Him.

You've got to measure *every single thing* according to the Word.

When you don't, think — that is quitting.

Yielding to an undisciplined life is quitting.

It's not what happens to you that counts; it's what you do with what happens to you that, counts.

Anything you can do to move the Word is your absolute minimum responsibility.

I don't think great wisdom comes with age; it comes with believing.

There is one way to get started in anything and that is to *start*.

God bless you. I love you. You are the best.

"Our people need to get their heads in the Word— first thing in the morning."
Dr. Victor Paul Wierwille

1 Thessalonians 5:23, 24

And the very God of peace sanctify you wholly; and *I pray God* your whole spirit and soul and body be preserved blameless unto the coming of our Lord Jesus Christ.

Faithful *is* he that calleth you, who also will do *it.*

Mrs. Dorothea Wierwille (Left)
Dr. V. P. Wierwille (Right)

Mrs. Dorothea Wierwille

Keep in mind that God placed us where it pleased Him. If it pleased Him, let it please us too.

Adorn yourself with good works.

It's the spirit that quickeneth our mortal bodies.

It will take *you* to make up your mind to take this life that is more than abundant.

When you get to the point where you're ready to throw in the towel and quit, you've swerved from the Word and are walking by your senses.

We want to keep from mental anemia.

God's commitment to us is 100%.

When we bless others, we will receive a blessing. That's how a good day works.

Speaking in tongues does not take the place of renewed mind.

Exhaustion is caused by conflict and tension, not by responsibility.

Problems are a sort of perplexity and vexation, according to Webster's dictionary. But when we renew our minds to the Word, these problems are short-lived. You don't want to stay in a negative state because if you do, you're the loser.

Our walk is proof of whether we are believing or not.

We are not ever dependent on our surroundings because God is always there.

Dr. Wierwille has said, 'The least God can do is His Word.' The *most* He can do is according to your believing.

Our mind is like a computer. We want to hold truthful thoughts in our computer.

Where else could you learn so many truths that you could stake your life on?

You are the most important person in your life. — You are responsible for your actions.

When we walk tall, that whole armor of God won't rub.

Proverbs 31:10, 25

Who can find a virtuous woman? for her price *is* far above rubies.

Strength and honour *are* her clothing; and she shall rejoice in time to come.

H. E. Wierwille (Right)
Dr. V. P. Wierwille (Left)

H.E. Wierwille
Known affectionately as "Uncle Harry"

If you want a healthy body and sound mind, get your nose in the Book, DAILY.

When we read God's Word, it's God speaking to our minds.

No one is a failure.

We are spiritual partners.

Believing is the greatest horse sense in the world.

And God...Send people to us, so we can get more done, do less running around and in less time. — *Uncle Harry praying.*

We're God's professionals.

You've got to stand on something because it's no use to be kicked around all your life.

I'm just starting to realize the greatness of the Christ in me. When it starts to move, people get delivered.

When you start believing the Word, you extend your life line.

We run too much instead of believe.

No man is self-made. That is the biggest lie from hell. It is all the grace of God that we are what we are.

The higher you go, the humbler you become, the greater you can serve GOD.

Selling is in the last minute.

If you don't want to go to a meeting because you don't feel good, go out of respect for God and His Word. That way, you will learn....If I were younger, I would want to be a student here.

We'd rather be taken advantage of ten times than to take advantage of another once.

If you want a good crop, you've got to sow the right seed and enough of it.

Most people are selfish, just thinking of themselves; but giving is in all phases: time and money. You have to help someone else to pull yourself out.

Nobody has a better time than we do in The Way ministry — a little foolishness now and then is relished by the best of men!

The greatness of traveling around the Way Ministry is that they love you to life...we teach each one how to help himself and this is doing more than 23,000 letters a day!

Luke 14:28-30: 'For which of you, intending to build a tower, sitteth not down first, and counteth the cost, whether he have *sufficient* to finish *it?* Lest haply, after he hath laid the foundation, and is not able to finish *it,* all that behold *it* begin to mock him, Saying, This man began to build, and was not able to finish'. — Follow this scripture unless you have direct orders from God; here's your guide.

Ephesians 4:1

I therefore, the prisoner of the Lord, beseech you that ye walk worthy of the vocation where-with ye are called,

Donnie Fugit

Donnie Fugit
In the Fifth Corps

Action cures fear, BUT non-action strengthens fear.

As a household, we've got something not seen since the first century.

The Love of God is when it's time to hold forth the Word — you tell it like it is.

You never really understand freedom until you see, or know, or begin to understand the mystery of the one body.

The body of Christ functions most admirably when the mind of Christ is evident.

You never grow up till you renew your mind — it never happens till you do it.

Grace is an experience indescribably real. It is truly the only reality. It is so real that most people will not even come near to it.

Praise or worship and obedience make up a heart of love for God.

Mystery has melted our hearts in the Way Corps.

Love is always comforting.

Do you know why you bring so much pressure upon yourself? Because you don't freely apply knowledge.

The greatest thing that sets my day is to share my love with anyone early in the morning. Sweet love with a morning kiss starts a day of giving beautifully. I especially keyed in on Dr. Wierwille's great love for the Word, and just reading it and letting it speak. Not complicated, only glorious.

Speaking in tongues gives the heart beat... evidenced by the following entry: Thump, Thump, Thump....

Around here you have to put on your eagle eyes and elephant ears — and you'll get big and fat flying high.

I firmly believe the whole reason for the USA being here is The Way ministry and the Word of God that is taught and lives here. I also believe everyone that's here in the Corps, our whole lives, led up to the Corps.

We, as the Way Corps, especially are called to guard the knowledge of the Word that we have...and the way to guard it is to do it.

2 Timothy 2:1, 2

Thou therefore, my son, be strong in the grace that is in Christ Jesus.

And the things that thou hast heard of me among many witnesses, the same commit thou to faithful men, who shall be able to teach others also.

Grace Bliss

Grace Bliss

Our bodies are a gift from God — a very precious gift....Living as healthfully as you can is a vital part of being a Christian.

If you're an average person you're as far from the top as you are from the bottom.

You are what you eat!

Day after day our bodies should be bubbling with exuberance and health.

People are like pins. They lose their heads and they are no good.

The best things in life are free, and nothing is more free or more important than the air we breathe. — *By Grace*

Luxuries are the things that make people do without necessities. Let's always remember to keep the necessities.

Next to God's Word, the greatest thing He ever put together was the human body. Doctors and scientists know so little about it compared to what God knows. The human body is a very complex organism; but if we treat it right, it will treat us right.

Leviticus 17:11
For the life of the flesh *is* in the blood:...

Others

Christian etiquette manifests itself in every move that you make. It's when you are unobserved that your attitude really shows up.
— *Dorothy Owens*

We cannot expect the God of Truth to be with us if we neglect the truth of God.
— *Gail Winegarner*

That which you have saved for yourself is lost. That which you have spent on others is saved. — *Indian Proverb, Orientalism Dept.*

Anybody throwing dirt automatically loses ground. — *Francis Winkowitsch*

You know, a pig don't give up! — *George Jess*

Sin is simply falling short of the will of God.
— *Frances Winegarner*

You can't know the *God of Truth* until you know the Truth of God's Word.
— *Gail Winegarner*

You can't separate obedience from believing.
— *Gail Winegarner*

If you mean business with respect to the Word, then you'll make a covenant of salt with God to be faithful to that which you have been taught. — *Bishop Pillai*

Christians have crossed the Red Sea to salvation, but some of us are still wandering in the wilderness because we haven't crossed the Jordon to the Promised Land. When God says jump, we jump. It's *His* problem where we're going to land. The Spaniards came for gold, the Pilgrims came for God and the Pilgrims got the land. When the pupil is ready, the teacher will appear. — *Gail Winegarner*

The Constitution does not say that we will be provided for. It says it will provide for our protection. — *Milford Bowen*

Develop your ability to be specific — *Bill Maize*

You are not in a situation of criticism, you are in a situation of learning. — *Bill Maize*

We have problems relating to people because we don't give them the benefit. — *Bill Maize*

Even if you're on the right track, you'll get run over if you just sit there. — *Will Rogers*

I firmly believe that any man's finest hour —
his greatest fulfillment to all he holds dear
— is that moment when he has worked his
heart out in *a* good cause and lies ex-
hausted on the field of *battle* — victorious.
                                    — *Vince Lombardi*

The truth is believed because it is the truth.
                                    — *Gert Behenna*

Realizing that our commitment is a result of
God placing in us desire to love Him. We're
so complete. — *Helen Parker*

Habit both shows and makes the man, for it
is at once historic and prophetic, the mirror
of the man as he is and the mould of the
man as he is to be.
        — *Arthur T. Pierson,* author of *George Muller of Bristol*

The excitement in obedience is finding out
later what God had in mind. — *God's Smuggler*

Do not limit the avenue by which God will
answer prayers. Remember that God's way
of manifesting His love are as uncountable
as the stars of the firmament. — *Glen Clarke*

To ask has value. To decide upon the answer
has greater value. To act upon the decision

is of supreme importance, whether the decision acted upon be good, bad, or indifferent. It is better to keep busy with blunders and mistakes, trials and errors than it is to sit with folded hands and a heart filled with unexpressed and frustrated wishes. — *Starr Daily*

The beautiful thing about the doctrine of love is that it casts out all fear, all striving and struggling. You merely act and express the virtues and qualities of love, and all that is needed to sustain you in happiness and harmony are inevitable consequences of your action. You are attached to nothing except the action of love. You desire no results; but possess perfect assurance that the correct results necessary to your life at a given time will be supplied: the sense of impending insecurity is unknown to him who lives the doctrine of love. — *Starr Daily*

He who shall introduce into public affairs the principles of primitive Christianity will revolutionize the world. — *Benjamin Franklin*

I press toward the mark for the prize of the high calling of God in Christ Jesus.

— *Paul the Apostle*

It is impossible to rightly govern without God and the Bible. — *George Washington*

The difference between the right word and *almost* the right word is the difference between lightning and the lightning bug.

— *Mark Twain*

Made in the USA
San Bernardino, CA
13 February 2018